nature's friends

Spiders

by Ann Heinrichs

Science Adviser: Terrence E. Young Jr., M.Ed., M.L.S., Jefferson Parish (La.) Public Schools

Content Adviser: Jan Jenner, Ph.D.

Reading Adviser: Dr. Linda D. Labbo, Department of Reading Education, College of Education, The University of Georgia

COMPASS POINT BOOKS

MINNEAPOLIS, MINNESOTA

Compass Point Books
3109 West 50th Street, #115
Minneapolis, MN 55410

Visit Compass Point Books on the Internet at *www.compasspointbooks.com*
or e-mail your request to *custserv@compasspointbooks.com*

Editor: Patricia Stockland
Photo Researcher: Marcie C. Spence
Designer: The Design Lab

Library of Congress Cataloging-in-Publication Data
Heinrichs, Ann.
  Spiders / by Ann Heinrichs.
        p. cm. — (Nature's friends)
Includes bibliographical references (p.   ).
ISBN 0-7565-0590-9 (hardcover)
1. Spiders—Juvenile literature. I. Title. II. Series.
QL458.4.H46 2004
595.4'4—dc22   2003014436

Table of Contents

NOTE: In this book, words that are defined in the glossary are in **bold** *the first time they appear in the text.*

Nature's Weavers

Take a walk on a summer morning. You might see brand-new spider webs in the grass. Spiders made them during the night. Spiders are amazing creatures. They spin silky threads and weave fantastic webs.

There is a Greek **myth** about how spiders began. Arachne was a weaver who wove beautiful designs. The goddess Athena was jealous and tore up Arachne's work. Arachne died of sadness. Then Athena was sorry. She changed Arachne into a spider, so Arachne could keep weaving forever.

In a way, Arachne is still at work. Spiders are called **arachnids** in the science world. Let's explore these amazing weavers. You'll see how they live and work—and how they help us, too!

◀ *A garden spider in a dewy web*

Spiders Around the World

Spiders have been on Earth a long time. They lived here almost 400 million years ago!

Spiders live everywhere on Earth except Antarctica. Some spiders live in the water. Most live on land. Spiders live in bushes, trees, or tall grass. Some live inside caves or buildings. Look in a closet or under a sofa. You might find spiders there, too!

The Samoan moss spider, or *Patu Marplesi,* is the world's smallest spider. It is just 0.017 inches (0.43 millimeters) long. That's smaller than the period at the end of this sentence.

The world's largest spider is the Goliath bird-eating tarantula. It lives in South America. Its legs stretch out more than 10 inches (25 centimeters). That's almost as wide as this page!

The Goliath bird-eating tarantula ▶

What Is a Spider?

You might think of a spider as a kind of insect. However, spiders are not insects at all.

Insects have six legs and two antennae, or feelers. Spiders have eight legs and no feelers. Each of a spider's eight legs has six joints. That means a spider has 48 knees!

Both spiders and insects have an exoskeleton. This is hard skin that protects the body and helps the spider to move.

Spiders produce thin threads called silk. Some weave it into fantastic webs. The webs are great food traps! They catch insects and other **prey** for the spider to eat. Most spiders eat insects. Some even eat small animals such as birds or frogs.

◄ *A green lynx spider rests on a thistle.*

A Spider's Body

A spider's body has two sections, or parts—the cephalo-thorax and the abdomen. A tiny waist called the pedicel joins the two sections.

The cephalothorax is the front part. It holds the brain, jaws, stomach, leg attachments, and eyes. Most spiders have eight eyes. They come in two rows of four eyes each. Other spiders may have six, four, or two eyes. Above the mouth are two chelicerae. The spider uses them like arms to grab prey. Each chelicera has a pointy fang on the end. On each side of the mouth is a pedipalp. They look like small legs. Both male and female spiders use them for eating. Males also use their pedipalps in reproducing.

The abdomen is the back part. It holds the spider's heart and breathing parts. At the end of the abdomen are spinnerets. These small, finger-like parts **secrete** the silk.

The underside of an orb weaver spider shows where the smaller cephalothorax and the larger abdomen meet. ▶

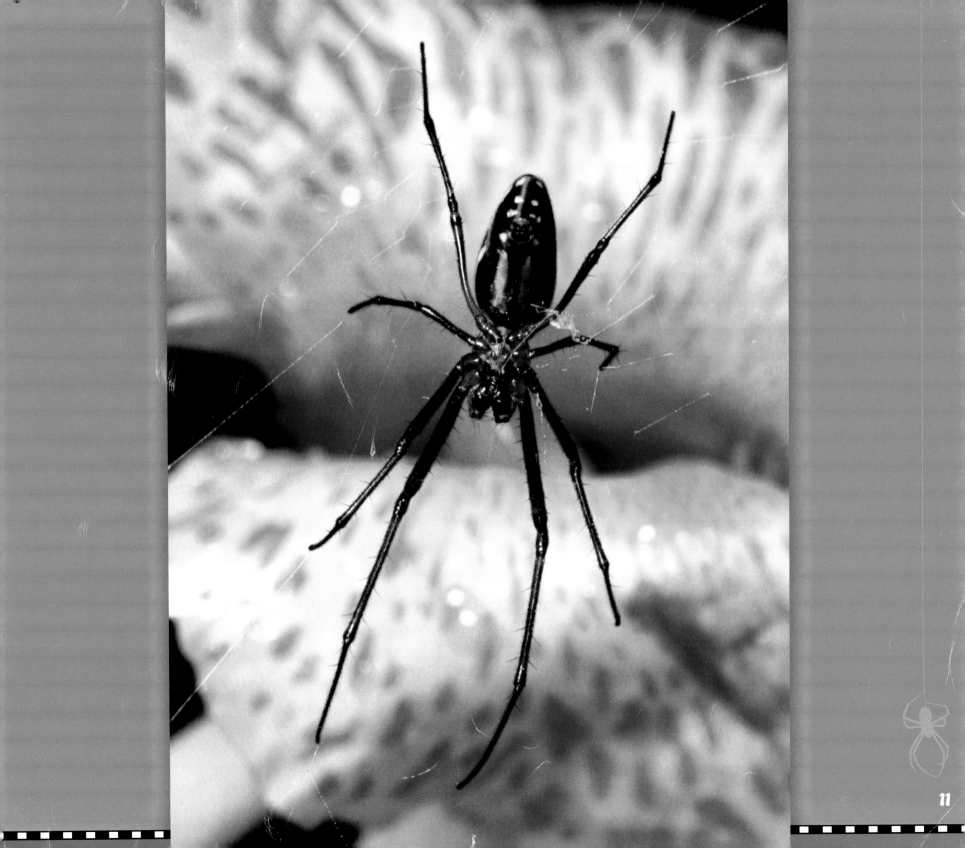

Life as a Spider

A male spider looks for a female mate. First, he must get her attention. He may wiggle her web or bring her a fly.

In mating, the male transfers **sperm** to the female. Then she lays her eggs. She may lay hundreds or even thousands of eggs. She spins a silk egg sac to hold them. Egg sacs come in different shapes. They might be round like a ball or slightly flattened.

Baby spiders are called spiderlings. They hatch inside the sac. After a while, they leave it. As they grow, they molt several times. That means they shed their exoskeletons and grow bigger ones.

A spider may live only a year or two. However, some **captive** tarantulas live more than 20 years!

◀ *A wolf spider waits near her egg sac while the spiderlings come out.*

Spinners and Hunters

Many spiders are web spinners. They make webs to catch their food. Other spiders are hunters. The jumping spider is a hunter. It chases its prey and pounces on it. Some jumping spiders can jump 50 times their own length.

Tarantulas are hunters, too. They are the world's biggest spiders. Trap-door spiders live in a tunnel, or tube, in the ground. They make a sort of lid at the top. When an insect comes near the lid, the spider darts out from the lid to grab it.

The crab spider ambushes its prey, or catches it by surprise. It lies in wait, maybe hiding in a flower. When an insect comes by, the spider jumps out and grabs it. Most ambush hunters are camouflaged. That means they match their surroundings.

A trap-door spider comes out of hiding to catch a beetle. ▶

Kinds of Webs

Can you draw an **orb** web? It looks like a wheel with lines running out from the center. Many threads of silk connect the lines together. Common garden spiders are orb weavers.

Some spiders are sheet-web weavers. Their webs are flat sheets of woven silk. They are usually found close to the ground. You might see a sheet web hanging between blades of grass. Funnel-web spiders build similar webs. In the center is a funnel, or tunnel. The spider hides there. When an insect lands in the web, the spider runs out to eat it.

Cobweb spiders, including American house spiders, often live in buildings—like your house! Their webs have no special design. They look like a tangled mess.

◀ *A funnel web covered in dew*

Spinning Webs and Catching Prey

Suppose you were spinning a web. How would you begin? An orb weaver begins with one silky thread. A breeze carries one end across to a spot where it sticks.

The next thread hangs down from the middle of the first thread. Together they form the letter *Y*. Now the spider can spin all the other threads.

Once the web is built, it's time to catch some food. The web shakes when an insect lands in it. That's how spiders know it is mealtime. Spiders grab their prey with their chelicerae. They sink their fangs in. The fangs inject venom. This substance usually stuns or kills the prey. Some venom simply helps spiders eat. The venom turns the insect's muscles and organs into liquid mush.

Spiders cannot eat solid food. They cannot chew. Instead, they suck in their food.

A spider prepares to eat a grasshopper trapped in its web. ▶

So Many Ways to Use Silk

All spiders spin silk. It is stretchy, sticky, and strong. Silk is good for many things besides webs. Most spiders make nests with their silk. Some spiders use silk to wrap up their prey.

Silk is good for keeping safe, too. As a spider walks along, it spins a silk thread behind it. This thread is called a dragline. If an enemy comes along, the spider swings away on its dragline.

Silk also helps the spider travel. It spins a thread of silk, and the wind catches it, like a kite or balloon. The wind carries the spider far away. This way of traveling is called ballooning. Sailors have seen ballooning spiders far out at sea.

◀ *A garden spider hangs on a dragline.*

Are Spiders Really Dangerous?

Will spiders bite? Just remember—spiders are afraid of *you*. To a spider, you look like a giant!

Spiders are not interested in biting people. They only bite if they feel they are in danger. Most spider bites are no worse than mosquito bites. The bitten spot may hurt, itch, or swell up.

Only a few spiders are truly dangerous to humans. One is the black widow. It has a red hourglass-shaped mark on its abdomen. The brown recluse spider is dangerous, too. It has a violin-shaped design on its back. Bites from these spiders can be very painful. They can make a person sick. However, such bites are rarely deadly.

The black widow can be dangerous to humans. ▶

Science and Spider Silk

Long ago, people used spider silk for healing. They spread the silk across cut or burned skin. Then the skin healed quickly.

Even today, scientists say spider silk is awesome. Imagine a thread made of steel as thin as spider silk. The silk is actually many times stronger than the steel! Spider silk can stretch like a rubber band. Then it springs right back without breaking.

Scientists are trying to make **artificial** spider silk. It could make strong fishing lines—or even seat belts or bulletproof clothing! Doctors could use the silk to sew up cuts. They could also make artificial body parts with it. As you see, spider silk has a great future!

◄ *This spider's silk is stronger than threads of steel.*

Our Spider Friends

Spiders may look a little scary. They are good friends to humans, though. Spiders help us by eating insects. Those insects can destroy a farmer's crops. They can also ruin a pretty garden. Insects such as mosquitoes bite us and our pets.

It's amazing to watch a spider weave a web. Spider silk is even more amazing. It can lead to many helpful discoveries.

When you see a spider, be careful. You may scare the spider when you don't mean to. The best rule is look, but don't touch. Remember, spiders are friends that help us all!

A jumping spider is our friend. ▶

Glossary

arachnids—a class of animals that includes spiders, scorpions, and mites

artificial—human-made; manufactured

captive—kept in a cage or locked up in some way

myth—an old story that helps people understand the natural world

orb—an object shaped like a circle

prey—an animal hunted by another animal for food

secrete—to release or give off

sperm—fluid from a male that fertilizes a female's eggs

Let's Look at Spiders

Kingdom: Animalia

Phylum: Arthropoda

Class: Arachnida

Order: Araneae

Suborder: Most common spiders belong to suborder Araneomorphae. Tarantulas belong to suborder Mygalomorphae.

Family: There are 108 families of spiders worldwide. More than 60 families live in the United States.

Species: There are more than 34,000 species of spiders worldwide. About 3,500 species live in the United States and Canada.

Range: Spiders live everywhere in the world except the continent of Antarctica. Most spiders live on land, but some live in the water.

Life span: Most spiders live one to two years. Some tarantulas can live for many years.

Life stages: Females lay batches of eggs and wrap them in sacs made of silk. Spiderlings hatch inside the sac and leave it. As they grow, they shed their exoskeletons several times until they reach adult size.

Food: Spiders eat insects as well as other spiders. Some spiders may eat small animals.

Did You Know?

The bolas spider spins one long strand of silk with a sticky ball on the end. The spider swings the strand of silk round and round. The sticky ball sticks to an insect. Then the spider reels it in and eats it.

Some spiders eat their web at the end of the day. Then they build a new web the next morning.

The golden orb web spider may spin webs more than 20 feet (6 meters) from top to bottom. They can catch small birds. People even use these webs to catch fish!

Spiders are the "highest" land animals on Earth. Mountain climbers found spiders at 22,000 feet (6,710 meters) on Mount Everest, the world's tallest peak.

A grassy field can have 1 million spiders per acre (.4 hectare).

West Africa has many spider legends. One legend tells how spiders taught people to weave cloth. Other tales tell about Anansi, a very tricky spider.

Arachnophobia means fear of spiders.

Junior Arachnologists

Arachnologists are scientists who study spiders and other arachnids. You can be an arachnologist, too! You will need a notebook, a pen or pencil, and a magnifying glass. Go outside, and look for spider webs. Some good places to look are in bushes and tall grass. If you don't have a big backyard, ask an adult to take you to a nearby nature center or wooded area. When you find a web, don't get too close to it. Use your magnifying glass to take a closer look. Be very careful not to disturb the spider if there is one in the web. Draw a picture of the spider web in your notebook. Make a note of any insects trapped in the web. Look for any holes where an insect may have torn free from the web. Sit very quietly and watch the spider for three minutes. Then move on and look for another web. Observe at least five webs, and record your observations in your notebook.

Now try to answer these questions:

How many different kinds of spider webs did you see? What kind of webs were they—orb, sheet, funnel, or cobweb?

What color were the spiders that you saw?

Were there any egg sacs?

Was there any prey wrapped in silk?

What kinds of insects were trapped in the spiders' webs?

How many different kinds of spiders did you see? How were they different from one another? How were they the same?

Did any spiders that looked different from one another spin the same kind of web?

Draw a picture of one of the spiders you saw.

Want to Know More?

AT THE LIBRARY

Allen, Judy, and Tudor Humphries. *Are You a Spider?* New York: Kingfisher, 2000.

Parsons, Alexandra, and Jerry Young (photographer). *Amazing Spiders.* New York: Knopf, 1990.

Sill, Cathryn P., and John Sill (illustrator). *About Arachnids: A Guide for Children.* Atlanta: Peachtree, 2003.

ON THE WEB

For more information on **spiders,** use FactHound to track down Web sites related to this book.

1. Go to *www.compasspointbooks.com/facthound*
2. Type in this book ID: **0756505909**
3. Click on the *Fetch It* button.

Your trusty FactHound will fetch the best Web sites for you!

ON THE ROAD

Dallas Museum of Natural History
3535 Grand Ave.
Fair Park
Dallas, TX 75315
214/421-3466
To see exhibits of live spiders in their natural habitats

THROUGH THE MAIL

Smithsonian Institution Office of Education
National Museum of Natural History
Constitution Avenue and 10th Street N.W.
Washington, DC 20560
202/357-2700
For more information on spiders

Index

About the Author: Ann Heinrichs grew up in Fort Smith, Arkansas. She began playing the piano at age three and thought she would grow up to be a pianist. Instead, she became a writer. She has written more than 100 books for children and young adults. Several of her books have won national awards. Ms. Heinrichs now lives in Chicago, Illinois. She enjoys martial arts and traveling to faraway countries.